The Swinging Sixties?
A Year in our Lives

Jean Wolfendale

Contents

Chapter One

The Idea

Spring, 1961, the days before computers, faxes or modems. Most women with children stayed at home, at least until they started school. Play groups were in their infancy and state nursery provision was scanty. Private nurseries were few and far between. In the days before Community Charges, before Poll Tax, Rates were payable twice a year. For a young couple with a growing family, the bills became ever more difficult to settle.

This particular year, the garden looked delightful, the bulbs were in full bloom and the trees just coming into blossom. However, the bright spring sunshine, lighting every corner of the house, reminded us forcibly of the many defects in our decorations and furniture.

"The twins will soon start school. I'll get a job", I proposed.

"No", replied my husband. "Part time jobs are hard to find, and we wouldn't want the children to come home to an empty house. However, perhaps we could move to the country; the rates are cheaper outside the towns."

Then THE IDEA occurred to me.

"Let's buy a country store!"

Together we detailed the advantages; the children would have lots of fresh air and exercise; I could run the shop and yet be at home when the children returned from school; the cost of living would be cut as we would buy everything wholesale and there should be little or no competition (for we knew little or nothing of shop keeping). In the country we should be able to find the large living accommodation and garden we required for ourselves and our three children. This was long before the days of supermarkets, when corner shops and country stores still flourished.

The search was on! Every weekend we piled into the car armed with lists of desirable properties. We had limited our search to within thirty miles of Sheffield, so that we should not cut ourselves off completely from our relatives and friends. We felt sure that within such an area we could find the right place for us. Every weekend, however, we climbed wearily out of the car again. This one was too small, that one too far from school. Another needed extra staff whom we may or may not have been able to pay. Nearly all were much too expensive.

Our only capital was the profit we hoped to make on the sale of our semi-detached house that we had bought on our marriage eight years previously, and a hundred or two in the bank. As banks will not lend money for the purchase of stock or 'goodwill', we were necessarily limited in price.

We were very much tempted by one place we visited. Approached by a winding wooded lane leading down to a bridge over a river, it was a converted water mill. Part of the big mill wheel remained outside, and across the ceiling inside ran the huge tree-trunk which had conveyed the motive power to the grindstone. The inside had been converted into a cafe and small shop selling mainly ice creams and soft drinks. The present owners ran the business very satisfactorily with the help of their four children, but these were responsible teenagers, not little ones like mine. With the river close by, it was no place for children to play unsupervised and as at times the cafe became exceptionally busy, we reluctantly decided it was not for us.

The summer was at its height when we drove into one small village, almost on the edge of our thirty mile limit. It was rather difficult to find, and several times we almost turned back. This was the last name on our list for the time being, so we kept on a little longer and at last drew to a halt outside Prospect Stores.

From the outside it looked most inviting. A double-fronted shop faced on to the village street, with a side entrance to the living quarters around the corner. It certainly lived up to its name, for it had a glorious view across a well-wooded green valley. In front of the house was a small garden full of roses, while to one side a long drive, bordered by a blaze of dahlias and hollyhocks in full bloom led to garage and garden. This latter garden was roughly half an acre in extent and so fertile that rhubarb came up to my eye level and the Brussels sprouts seemed like young trees.

Inside, the shop was equally intriguing. It was quite large, but it gave the impression of being small, owing to the dark paint and the lines strung across the ceiling bearing men's trousers, dusters, clothes lines and other strange items.

The store appeared to sell everything. Groceries,

frozen food, clothes pegs, knitting wool, baby clothes, firewood, wellington boots, bird seed, shampoo and pudding basins were jumbled together in seemingly hopeless confusion.

As we entered the shop, the owner appeared and invited us into the living quarters behind. We were too polite to give more that a cursory glance into corners, but after some of the cramped accommodation we had recently seen, these rooms were certainly spacious and had "possibilities".

A large farmhouse kitchen opened from the back of the shop. The fact that it had no heating escaped our notice. We were too busy exclaiming on its size and convenience. Along the garden side of the house ran a huge living room. It was roughly twenty-seven feet by fifteen feet, plus a dining alcove of at least ten feet square. The room was lit by two large windows and from it the front door opened directly into the garden. In one corner was a large, box-like structure, reaching to the ceiling.

"What is that?" we asked.

"It is the ice-cream kiosk", we were told.

Somewhat taken aback, we went over to look and saw that it enclosed a small window giving on to the street, from which ice cream could be dispensed when the shop itself was closed.

This lounge was also connected to the shop by means of a dim, dark stockroom, giving a circular plan to the ground floor of the house. Also from the stockroom a twisty, rickety stairway led to the bedrooms. Although in an appalling state of decoration, these were convenient and again had possibilities. We took particular note of the two boxrooms, one of which would make a grand home for my husband's beloved electric train layout.

The bathroom had been well modernised, there were four large bedrooms and a further, well-lit staircase that led down into the kitchen.

No sooner had the children discovered the possibilities of this than they were off, and the house was soon ringing to their laughter as they chased up one stair, down the other and through kitchen and lounge. Fortunately the owners liked children, having four of their own, so we took advantage of the respite to discuss financial arrangements. As the property was freehold and the owners were prepared to leave a certain sum on deferred payment, it seemed possible that we could just about meet the price.

We asked how the shop was heated. "Oh, we have central heating", they said, and proudly showed us the gleaming radiators in the shop. "The boiler is in the cellar. It only needs attention once a day, but I won't take you down there now, the stairs are dark and dusty." How we wished later that we had risked the dark stairs and inspected the boiler.

As we drove home, the children steadily munching their way through the pile of sweets and biscuits given them by their new friends, we eagerly discussed the property. It seemed to fulfil most of our conditions. It was near to schools, the living accommodation, though in a very bad decorative state, was certainly big enough, and the job was one with which I could cope single-handed.

"We'll move in September", we planned. Little did we know the ways of solicitors. We had decided to do all this in the middle of a credit squeeze. The banks were very sticky about allowing us a mortgage, and, worst of all, our beautiful house, which in spite of our dissatisfaction really was in excellent order, proved very difficult to sell. All around us other properties were sold, but not ours. Autumn drew into winter, one removal date was made, only to be cancelled because the other people's house was not ready, but finally arrangements were made for us to move on December 12th.

Our plans had met with a wonderful reception from our families. They must have had very grave doubts of our ability to cope with such an undertaking, knowing how inexperienced and impecunious we were, but they concealed these admirably and gave us all the help and support they could.

For two Saturdays prior to moving day I visited the shop for the day in order to gain some little experience. I was horrified. There was so much to learn. Where were things kept? Above all, how do I know what to charge? Our kind predecessors did their best to label as much as possible of the stock on the shelves, but being very busy with preparations for their own move, they soon gave up. They did, however, introduce me to an invaluable little booklet known as "Shaw's" which listed all the retail prices of groceries. (This was in the days of Retail Price Maintenance.) I took this book to bed with me every night and tried to learn its contents by heart. I was quite unsuccessful, but did at least become familiar enough with its pages to find a price very quickly. It was to be my constant companion for months. The pricing of the drapery was very much trial and error. Very little of it was labelled, and until invoices for new stock started coming in, I just had to make a wild guess.

One of my biggest worries was the 'Bread Book'. Would I ever be able to understand it? This was a long, thin book, ruled into columns for the days of the week, which was full of such strange symbols as 'Mrs. Manton. T. Th.Sat. M.P. 1 MC, 1BC.' This contained the customers' bread requirements and had to be written up each morning and handed to the bakers' roundsman when he called. In such a small community all bread was ordered and we carried only about half a dozen spare loaves for 'casuals'.

I returned home from these 'training sessions' utterly weary after standing all day, but elated at the fun of learning something new, and meeting people after nearly eight years of domesticity.

Chapter Two

Preparing for the Move

At last the great day arrived. The previous owner's furniture was to be moved out on the Saturday. On that day also, we should count and price every item of stock in the establishment – all this on a busy day three weeks before Christmas. Our own furniture was to arrive on the Monday.

We arranged for our three children to stay with their long-suffering grandparents for the weekend, enrolled the help of my uncle who was experienced in the grocery trade, and set off early on Saturday morning.

"We'll start counting in the stock room, so as to leave the shop clear during the busiest part of the day", I arranged with the departing owners.

I fetched a stool and disappeared into the depths at the back of the stock-room.

"Two garden forks, six large flower pots, one firegrate. Twelve tins brass polish. Six cases of disinfectant (thirty-six in each), forty-three tins of talcum powder, ten packets of slug killer."

Soon we started to cough. I looked round and saw clouds of smoke billowing out from a closed door behind us.

"It's all right – we've just lit the boiler", we were assured. "It'll clear very soon."

It did, but not before everything in the stockroom was covered in another film of dust to add to the several layers already there.

"Why on earth haven't they put these in the dustbin?" I whispered to my uncle, as I tripped for the twentieth time over one of the dozens of empty sweet jars that littered the floor.

"Because they are worth two shillings each", he replied. "We must count them all, and you must pay for them." Later, it took us almost six months to get all those jars back to their rightful owners and reclaim our two shillings on each one.

Lunch was taken on two packing cases in the empty lounge. Without its furniture, this looked most depressing. My husband had an idea.

"I can't help with the stocktaking" (we had decided this was my job, as it was the quickest way of learning where things were kept), "so I'll strip the wallpaper off ready for decorating. It will be much easier to do it before our furniture arrives and with a bit of luck, I might have the whole room decorated in time for Christmas."

After lunch, my uncle and I returned to the stocktaking, leaving Geoff happily engaged with a bucket and scraper.

Now it was time to count the goods in the shop. Progress was very slow.

"Mrs. Wolfendale, come and meet Mrs. Harper. She is your new next door neighbour and a very good customer."

"Good afternoon, Mrs. Harper. I do hope you will carry on coming here. We'll do our very best to look after your wants."

"Of course I shall still come. I've been a customer of this shop since I was a girl." And she would launch into a full and frank discussion of all the previous owners to date. I found all this absolutely fascinating, but when repeated at regular intervals it certainly slowed down our progress. Of course, our arrival was an event of earth-shattering magnitude to this tiny village, and the sale of boxes of matches soared as the population came in to inspect us.

Wearily I remounted the stool. (Everything seemed to be on high shelves.)

"Twenty five tins of peaches, fourteen large tins of pears, eight tins of pineapple, twenty-nine small tins of fruit salad."

"Cross off one tin of peaches, dear, I've just sold it."

Now we were round to the knitting wool. This was packed in transparent cellophane bags, many of which had been opened at both ends, with the result that when I took them down from the shelf to count them, all the wool fell out, and we spent a great deal of time on our hands and knees retrieving it from among the various boxes which covered the floor.

"Eight ounces blue double knitting wool. Six ounces white three-ply, eighteen ounces pale blue quickerknit." All hopelessly jumbled together.

With a short break for tea we worked on all evening. At ten o'clock there only remained a set of small, brown-painted drawers behind the counter. "These shouldn't take long", I thought to myself. At midnight we were still counting.

"Nine dozen and three boxes of razor blades."

"Twenty-eight boxes of chalks."

"Sixty-four packets of iron-on patches", (these were 2/6d each).

"Three hundred and eighty-six buttons."

"Fifty-one small bottles of aspirin" – and enough patent medicines to keep the whole village going for the next six years.

Finally there was one drawer left. "We'll make you a present of those", said the departing owners, anxious to be on their way. "How generous", we thought. 'They' were a collection of twelve nutcrackers. We never sold one, and they were passed on, intact, to the next owners.

Just after midnight we wearily put down our pens and trooped into the lounge. There sat my husband on an up-turned crate, gazing dejectedly at the wall.

We too gazed, horrified. As he had pulled off the wallpaper, the plaster had come away with it and we were looking at the rough stone blocks that formed the external walls of the cottage.

Thus ended our first day in our new home.

We returned to our old house for one more night, but next morning we set off once more for the shop, this time taking with us our cat, Tipsy. The journey proved quite hilarious, as he escaped from the improvised basket in which I was carrying him and wandered about the car, several times attempting to squeeze through the spokes of the steering wheel. I eventually managed to recapture him and he settled down fairly well on my lap, from which he could look out of the window.

Arrived at the shop, we made Tipsy as comfortable as possible in the warmest corner of the cold and draughty living room (we could see daylight through the cracks between the stones) and settled down to the mammoth job of pricing the stock.

My uncle found no major difficulties with the groceries beyond the actual mathematics of working out, say fifty-nine tins of tomatoes at two pounds for a case of forty-eight. (This was long before the days of calculators!) However, when we came to the less usual items, such as 'Hot-water bottles (soiled)', or '32 pairs children's socks', we just made an inspired guess. Much of the time, as we subsequently discovered, we guessed on the high side. Naturally enough the vendors did not feel it necessary to enlighten us!

We plodded doggedly on, and by tea time a total had been reached and agreed. The keys were handed over. The shop was ours!

Now was to occur the first of my ordeals. Geoff had to return to Sheffield to take home my weary uncle and to supervise the loading of our furniture on the morrow. Someone, however, had to be on hand to open the shop at eight o'clock next morning, so it had been arranged that I was to stay the night at the shop – alone! We had brought a camp bed and blankets with us, so after saying goodbye to my husband and expressing our heartfelt thanks to my hardworking uncle, I double locked and bolted all doors and took stock of my surroundings.

Although it was already nine o'clock, my first thought was to attempt to clean up the rooms before the arrival of children and furniture next day. The two rooms we had earmarked for the children were over the lounge and had windows overlooking the garden. Originally one large room, it had been divided by a hardboard partition, making two good sized double bedrooms. However, it had been done in such a way that it was necessary to step into Janet's room before turning right into the boys' room. This was to lead to many arguments later. If the boys had teased her or upset her in some way, Janet would slam her bedroom door, saying 'You can't come into my bedroom' – at which John or Peter would come running to me in the shop and, heedless of any customer who might be present complain, "Mummy we want to go into our room and Janet won't let us". Customers were very understanding and would always say, "Go and sort them out, Mrs. W. I don't mind waiting a few minutes."

However, all this was in the future.

This particular evening, I wearily climbed the stairs, bucket in hand. Janet's room wasn't too bad. I hastily mopped the floor, washed the window and called it clean. In the boy's room was a hardboard panel rather insecurely fastened to the wall. I had wondered what its purpose was, but had been too polite to ask. Now I eased one corner away from the wall. Horrors! It concealed a fireplace – not the ordinary bedroom fireplace, but a very dilapidated type of Yorkshire range. Perhaps in its prime, with plenty of black-lead lovingly applied, it may have been attractive (and today would no doubt fetch a fortune as an antique) but then its rust and dirt horrified me. The central grate was full of coke and ash and the two side hobs were at least two inches deep in dust. Hurriedly I fetched brush and shovel and cleared away the worst of the mess, then hastily pushed the panel back into place again with a shudder at the thought of my two dear little boys sleeping near such a thing. Little did I know the uses to which it would be put in the future.

Hastily mopping over the bathroom, I left the spare room and two boxrooms severely alone. The spare room, for some reason, had a brownstone sink in one corner and across the room another hardboard panel looking rather as though it might conceal another monstrous fireplace. I didn't investigate.

One of the boxrooms boasted a drawing of a motor-cyclist on its distempered walls. This quite skilful piece of work must have measured at least four feet by two feet. The other walls were adorned by 'No smoking' and 'Bus stop' signs – metal ones. Some of the previous owners had had unusual tastes in decoration. Still another boxroom was piled high with boxes and boxes of paper bags and birthday cards.

For the moment I dismissed these from my mind and moved on to our own bedroom. This was to be the room over the shop, which boasted two windows overlooking the street and was enormous. It dwarfed all the furniture we later put into it. The carpet, which had filled the bedroom of our previous home, looked like a postage stamp, and it seemed like a four-mile hike from door to bed. Tonight, however, it seemed like heaven after the cold rooms downstairs, for it boasted a gas fire and I had hung the curtains. It looked so welcoming after the glassy reflections downstairs. Hastily mopping over the floor, I flung down the mop and tumbled exhausted into bed.

I was not to sleep however. The house seemed to come alive at night, after the manner of old houses. Our bedroom had three doors, one to the landing, one to the bathroom and one to a large walk-in cupboard with its own window. All these doors were fitted with latches and all rattled if the merest breath of wind caught them. The sash windows also rattled, and downstairs the motors of the three fridges switched themselves on and off in a syncopated rhythm that made sleep impossible.

Chapter Three

Moving Day

I must finally have dozed off to sleep, for I was brought back to consciousness by a new noise that added itself to the orchestra. 'Tinkle, Tinkle, thrump, slam', accompanied by the noise of footsteps below the window. It was still pitch dark outside, but by the feeble light of one street lamp I could just see another shadowy figure approaching the wall of the shop. The noise came again – of course – the automatic cigarette machine. It must be the miners on early shift calling for cigarettes on their way to work. I snuggled down into bed listening happily, for every 'tinkle' meant another lovely half crown for our till.

I dozed for another hour till I was fully aroused by the shrilling of the alarm clock. Hastily dressing I proudly put on my new overall and went downstairs. After the warmth of the bedroom (I had rather extravagantly left the radiator burning all night), the kitchen seemed icy cold. I hurriedly plugged in the radiator that we had brought with us. After a quick cup of tea I transferred the radiator to the shop and proudly unlocked the door. I reversed the little card that read

'Not open even for Stamina' (a brand of dog food) to 'Open for Stamina'. We were ready for business.

My first caller arrived some five minutes later.

"Can I help you?" I enquired.

"No love," was the reply, "I'm the potted meat man. Eight and six please, and can I have the empty dish from last week?"

After a hurried search, the dish was finally located in the oven, containing the remains of a fish and chip lunch, presumably from the previous owners. The potted meat man departed and I settled down to write up the 'Bread Book'. This was causing me considerable worry. It had been explained to me that the various symbols represented different types of bread, but how was I to know who wanted what? I decided to trust to luck and copied out the previous Monday's list. At the back of the book I found a list headed 'Potted Meat' with various names and amounts, so I set to and weighed out and labelled the potted meat I had just bought.

Time hung heavily and, in spite of the radiator, I was cold. It was only 8.30 but I daren't go and light the boiler in case a customer came into the shop and I had to serve him with dirty hands. (In later months I would happily wield paint brush or duster during shop hours and customers would always say 'Of course I don't mind if you go to wash your hands. Take your time.') No one was in a hurry in the country.

Suddenly the door opened and the shop was full of children.

"Two ha'penny Bell Boys, please Missus."

"A penny gob-stopper, please."

"What have you got for twopence?"

They were on their way to school and as they made

their purchases they were all eyeing the new owner. 'Wonder what she's going to be like.' The little burst of activity left me breathless. I checked the till. I had taken precisely eleven pence.

Once again the village street was empty and I began to arrange the shelves in some kind of order. Cigarettes and matches went on small shelves immediately behind me as I stood at the counter. I filled these up and then found a piece of paper and my old friend 'Shaw's Guide', copied out the prices and pinned up the list. I moved along the shelves, sorting and tidying. Jams, honey – mincemeat? Suddenly I was conscious of deficiencies. No butter, no bacon, very little mincemeat, in fact, very little of anything else. Our predecessors had neglected to send in the weekly order to the wholesaler as they had promised. Hastily I telephoned. No, they couldn't deliver today, all their vans had already left. In desperation I phoned my husband. He had a friend who owned a grocer's shop and luckily carried some spare stock.

Thus it happened that our furniture van also delivered a side of bacon and various other groceries together with our household effects.

Now everything seemed to be happening at once. The bread was here, the children were here, the furniture was here.

Turning a deaf ear to the children's excited cries and leaving Geoff to cope with the furniture, I tried to sort out the bread order. I was to learn later that the roundsman, Jess, was a local institution, and he behaved true to form from the start.

"Don't you worry, Mrs. W. I'll make it right," he said as I endeavoured to explain my difficulties over the order. I didn't know what he meant, but took his

word as by now I was too busy to bother. The arrival
of Jess's brown and yellow van was obviously the signal
for which the housewives had been waiting, for now the
bell was ringing every few minutes.

"My bread please." Helplessly I turned to Jess,
who was stacking bread on the shelves.

"Morning, Mrs. Parkin", he said, without turning
round.

"One M.P. love" – handing it to me, "one and a
ha'penny" – in a lower voice. He finished stacking
bread and reappeared with a tray of tea-cakes and
'splits' – these latter were bread rolls, split, as their
name implied, filled with cream and coated with icing
sugar. I found out later that they tasted delicious,
but I mentally cursed them as I struggled to put them
into paper bags without getting my hands covered in
cream. (In those distant days the idea of handling
cakes with tongs, or even of keeping them covered was
still unheard of. Plastic wrappings were still a thing
of the future). Nevertheless, the cakes were almost all
sold within a few minutes and I struggled on in the shop
as Jess disappeared into the kitchen behind. Cigarettes
– where were they? "Just behind you love, and they're
one and eightpence ha'penny."

"My names Mr. Harris and I always have a milk
cob on Mondays, Thursdays and Saturdays. That's it
over there, and it's sixpence."

"A two-penny packet of custard powder, please
love. He wants it for his dinner."

At last a lull enabled me to follow Jess into the
kitchen. He had unearthed a stool and sat writing
up his order book. Geoff and the removal men stood
around him, chatting and drinking cups of tea, obvi-

ously from the steaming pot beside him. As I entered he poured out a cup of tea and handed it to me.

"I hope you don't mind. I reckoned you were busy and I always stop here for a cup."

Never was tea more welcome.

* * * *

The morning flew by. Geoff and the removal men performed wonderful gymnastic feats getting our furniture up the narrow stairs and all too soon it was lunch time. Ever resourceful, my husband produced a steaming newspaper full of fish and chips which we ate perched on boxes and stools in the kitchen. The removal men piled thankfully into their van and departed to the waves of the children with whom they had become bosom friends.

Now my immediate problem was to make the children's beds and this I accomplished in a series of hasty journeys up and down stairs. No sooner would I get the sheets and blankets assembled when 'ding' went the bell and I had to rush down to play 'Hunt the thimble' with another customer. All were most helpful and could tell me roughly the localities and price of the articles they needed. By tea-time I was feeling quite blasé, and when a customer came in saying, "A pint of vinegar, please," I proudly walked to the correct shelf and handed one over to her without hesitation.

"Oh, no, dear," she said, handing ME an empty bottle, "I want the loose sort."

"The loose sort?" I repeated blankly.

"Yes, she keeps it in the cellar."

There were two cellars to the shop, neither of which I had yet seen. One housed the boiler and was approached from the stockroom. It couldn't be that one, it was far too dirty. With dismay, I opened the forbidding-looking door that led off the lobby between shop and kitchen. A dim light bulb showed me the way down. On the bottom step, I stopped, appalled. A stone wall faced me, and the space between was piled high with cardboard boxes. Obviously our predecessors, when they had emptied a box, had just stood at the top of the steps and hurled it down. I pushed a few aside and turned the corner. The greater part of the floor was covered with bundles of wood, which appeared to have escaped from sacks piled in one corner. All around was rubbish of every description.

I glanced around. No sign of anything that could contain vinegar. Going back to the foot of the stairs, I turned the corner to the left, once more struggling past the mound of boxes. Here the mess was even more chaotic. Bird seed lay in small heaps on the floor. An accumulation of wire racks and sections of old shelving, dozens of empty bottles and jars of all shapes and sizes, and at last – oh yes – a barrel! This must be the vinegar.

Gingerly I approached. The top was covered with a mould-like substance, but there was a tap, which appeared clean. I was rewarded with a thin trickle that soon stopped. Conscious of the impatient customer above, I hastily tilted the barrel. Immediately a flood of vinegar spilled out, soaking my clean overall, my feet and spreading over the cellar floor. I finally managed a nice adjustment by tilting the barrel with one hand while holding the bottle with the other.

Triumphant, and smelling strongly of vinegar, I mounted the stairs to my customer. By now the shop was full.

"How much is the vinegar?" I asked.

"Eightpence" was the reply. For the effort involved, it should have been eight shillings!

We later found that most people preferred the cask vinegar and lost no time in ordering a new barrel, but my heart always sank at the request of 'Vinegar, please', and the prospect of another trip to that cellar.

The day wore on, and I began to assemble a collection of tins on the kitchen table to provide us with tea.

Once again the shop bell rang. This time it was someone I knew. My brother-in-law.

"I'm on my way to London", he explained, "and I felt I must call to see you."

In the confusion of removal, we had forgotten to tell him that our moving date had been postponed and he thought we had moved in a week previously. He had been travelling since early morning and was very tired and hungry.

"Nice to see you, Brian," I greeted him, "but I can't stop. You'll find a bed somewhere upstairs, and some blankets in a packing case. Go and make it up!"

Whilst the poor fellow was doing this I hastily prepared the tea, and at 6.30, thankfully closed the shop. Our first day as shopkeepers was over.

* * * *

Having done his best to organise the furniture and keep the children out of mischief, my husband had disappeared a little while previously. From the smoke that presently began to percolate around the house, I rightly concluded that he was lighting the boiler. On the call, "Tea's ready", he surfaced, hot, dirty and tired.

"I wanted to light the boiler tonight to save time in the morning", he explained, "but I can't get it to go."

Brian must have been horrified as he gazed round the living room. The gaps in the stone-work where the plaster had come off, the wall paper hanging in shreds where Geoff had stopped work, the hideous ice-cream kiosk in the corner and all our furniture piled higgledy-piggledy in the middle of the floor.

Geoff and I, however, were too excited to notice these minor irritations, and talked far into the night of the wonderful things we would do.

Chapter Four

Settling In

Next day we were up very early as my husband had to go back to work.

"I'll light the boiler before I go," he said "Don't forget to keep it stoked."

He disappeared into the cellar armed with a whole packet of firelighters and several bundles of firewood. Half an hour, and a lot of smoke later, he reappeared, triumphant.

"It's in," he said, and drove off, content, having done his good deed for the day.

Slowly the radiators in the shop began to glow with warmth and, deciding that this was the least chilly place, the children and I started refilling shelves and sorting once more.

All through our stay at the shop the sweet counter was naturally their especial delight, and they liked nothing better than to fetch the boxes from the stockroom and fill up the gaps on the shelves.

I had read somewhere that people who work in chocolate factories rapidly sicken of the sweets if allowed to eat their fill and after the first week or two never bother to take one. We decided to try this on the children. We gave them free rein, but soon found that they seemed to thrive on a diet of chocolate and rather than sickening, their appetites increased. Finally, after much argument, we settled on a daily allowance of three pennyworth of sweets, this being the smallest sum for which they could purchase an ice lolly.

Great competition soon developed however, as to who could get the most sweets with his threepence. The demand for Mojos at four a penny and tubes of small sherbet sweets at a penny a tube became enormous. Later on, demand for quantity was replaced to some extent by a taste for quality. Most of the sweets came in large jars and had to be weighed out. Because of our ruling, I was faced sometimes with the task of weighing out three pennyworth of sweets which cost, say eleven pence a quarter. When the twins started school their teacher was amazed at their grasp of simple money sums and weighing and measuring games. I was not.

This particular day, the children were quite absorbed in running back and forth with tins, packets and jars as I replenished and dusted the shelves. Every few minutes they would run to the door looking anxiously for Jess and the bread van. They had met him briefly the day before, but then there had been the excitement of the removal to occupy them. Now, when the brown and yellow van drew up at the door, Jess won their hearts completely with his easy manner as they helped him carry the trays of bread and cakes into the shop.

Jess did not arrive until 10.30 with the bread and from then until lunch time the shop was always busy. Once the children had passed on their way home from school, however, things seemed to be fairly quiet and I decided to close the shop so that we could have our own lunch in peace. From this time onwards, we closed for lunch every day, something our predecessors had never done, but custom did not seem to suffer by it. Knowing that on the morrow Janet would be home from school for lunch, I was determined to carry it on if at all possible.

By tea-time, we were all feeling very pleased with ourselves. Though still dark, gloomy and cluttered, the shelves were piled high with goods – at the expense of the stockroom which was almost empty. We were dreadfully understocked. It also looked much more orderly.

I was beginning to feel quite cold when suddenly I remembered – the boiler. Hastily I groped my way down the twisty stairs of the far cellar. One glance at the monster told me it had gone out long ago. Quickly raking it out, and adding fresh coke, I tried to relight it – but the shop bell recalled me. I had to leave it and confess failure to my husband when he returned.

Normally, Geoff's work took him away from home for two or three nights a week, but in this, our first week, he had arranged to come home every evening in order to help with the work of settling in. I am sure he rapidly regretted it as he battled each morning with that stubborn boiler.

Next morning brought a new hazard. Janet, our daughter, was to start at the village school. Our decision to move to the shop had not been made lightly. From the point of view of the twins it was an advantage as they would be able to start school a term earlier than at the overcrowded city school. Janet, however, was rather different. A highly intelligent child, she had the shyness that often goes with it, and at six and a half was just settling down and making friends at school. To uproot her now and start again at a new school would be quite a blow. However, after careful consideration we decided that the advantages for the family as a whole would compensate for this and the move had been made. Nevertheless, we wondered how she would settle down among the village children. My husband took her to school in the morning and I waited anxiously for her re-appearance at lunch time. Oh! the rush to have it on the table at exactly twelve o'clock. The shop bell always seemed to ring just as I was about to light the gas under the potatoes, or as the milk boiled over.

However, Janet settled down very happily at school. A few mornings in the early days were marred by tears at the thought of the lonely walk up the hill, but she soon made friends and the twins anxiously awaited Easter, when it would be their turn to start school.

* * * *

Crich, even in those days, was not a typical country village. It is now well known on two counts – for the tramway museum and as the setting for the TV serial 'Peak Practice'. In those days we knew that there was a group of people who pursued their hobby of tram repairing up in the old quarry. The site was not open to the public and had little impact on village life. The village is set amidst rolling hills, roughly six miles from any of the three towns that encircle it. The village church stood high on a hill, surrounded by a small group of cottages. At the foot of the hill was the market square, where four roads met. No market is held there these days, but the large square remains, bordered on one side by a group of shops. From the square the main street continues down the hill. Occasional shops are dotted along its length, and ours was one of these.

In the towns that surround the village, the chief industries were coal mining; the mills, where such things as nylon stockings were produced and the dye works, which dealt with raw wool from all over the country. In the village were two small housing estates. Most of the men worked either in the mines or the dye works, while many of the girls and women went to the mills. There were, of course, many productive farms, and we found that the agricultural population was cautious, clinging to old ideas, but always thrifty and hard-working. However, many of the industrial workers were much more happy-go-lucky, spending freely one minute and hard-up the next. The women, in particular, always had at the back of their minds the thought that if things got really tight, a week or two at one of the mills would soon put finances on an even keel again. It was an era of full employment and jobs were still fairly easy to find.

Like many country people, the population of our village was very religious and in addition to the church there were four chapels, each with its own loyal band of ardent supporters. Events such as May Day, or Harvest, went on for weeks, as each Chapel tried to arrange its celebrations so as not to clash with another. All these events were very well supported and we received warm invitations to attend them all. We did our best to do so, but with so many calls on our time, the best we could manage was an occasional appearance at church and the various school functions.

* * * *

By now it was the last weekend before Christmas.
We anxiously waited for Friday, the local pay day
which, we hoped, would be a day of bumper takings.
Little did we know the strange system on which our
customers worked. All through the week certain of
them had been coming into the shop, order book in
hand, collecting small supplies of goods and promising,
'I'll pay for these on Friday.' We had been warned by
our predecessors that this custom was quite usual and
nothing to worry about.

Early Friday morning our first customer appeared,
placing her order book on the counter. Eagerly I
assembled the goods and totalled the columns, after
much searching through price lists. Naturally I added
in the cost of the goods she had collected through the
week.

"That will be five pounds seven and fourpence
please", I said – our largest single order so far.

"Oh, no, ducks, I don't pay that, I'm starting again
today", said the customer, and turning back a couple
of pages in the order book showed me the total for the
previous week. I saw that it had not yet been marked
'paid'.

"This is what I pay today, look, Two pounds five
and six."

As I continued to look puzzled she explained.

"I always start again on Fridays. I'll pay you the
£5.7.4. next week."

By the time the next week came, she would owe
not only this amount but also the total of the goods
that she would send for through the coming week.

Dismayed, but naively trusting, I accepted her

word and added two pounds five shillings and sixpence to the till.

During the course of the morning I was to become more and more dismayed. Most of the customers brought in their orders, paid cash down and would have been shocked at the idea of any credit arrangement. However, a few, and those the biggest spenders, had this appalling credit system. They collected and sent for goods through the week on credit, then, when they had reached the limit of their housekeeping budget, they would happily draw a line under the total, announce they were 'starting again' and hope that they could pay the following week. The result was that they were soon several weeks in arrears.

Under this system the poor shopkeeper was helpless, since if he refused to serve them they would leave his outstanding bill unpaid and take their ready cash elsewhere. We later found that this credit system is rife in many poorer class areas in cities, but we had never met it before and I have certainly never heard of it flourishing to such an extent in the country.

However, this particular Friday, we were not aware of all these implications and the till tinkled away quite happily taking in the previous week's debts, whilst we innocently dished out baskets and baskets of goods to subsidise the Christmas of a good proportion of the village. Some of the debts incurred over Christmas were never repaid. Most were paid off at a few shillings a week.

The children were a great delight at this time as they came with sixpences and shillings to buy presents for their parents and siblings. It was a real test of ingenuity to provide them with something acceptable for a few coppers.

As I was quite unable to leave the shop, all our own Christmas presents that year were chosen from stock and some people received strange and varied gifts. Among the toys we had on display were two model cranes, a battery operated fire engine and a meccano set. The twins spent days of agony, as various people came and examined them, for they were longing to have them for themselves. I removed them from the shop just before Christmas and the children concluded in despair that they had been sold. Imagine their delight on Christmas morning when they opened their parcels to find these much coveted gifts.

On Saturday, my husband decided to finish stripping off the wall paper in the living room, preparatory to engaging a plasterer. While I raced to and fro in the shop, the children merrily helped in sloshing water on the wallpaper.

Saturday morning proved very busy in the shop. So much bread had been ordered that the kitchen table and cupboards had to be pressed into service – there wasn't sufficient room in the shop itself, and I flew back and forth to the now familiar tune of "Two cut, two cobs, two Hovis."

Saturday morning also saw the arrival of the greengrocer who called at the door with his lorry and while fulfilling my order bought twenty cigarettes and half a pound of mints. The butcher also sent his boy to enquire what I wanted and then delivered the meat half an hour later scantily wrapped in a very small square of paper. As we ourselves were very liberal in our use of bags, having inherited literally thousands, this never failed to annoy us.

Saturday afternoon was less busy and I took advantage of a temporary lull to look at the scene of activity in the living room. They had finally removed all the wallpaper and were having fun pulling down the ice-cream kiosk. We refused to open on Sundays. We could sell ice-cream from the shop every other day. It seemed pointless to leave it there.

I turned away from this scene of activity and my attention was caught by the fireplace, which seemed to be tilted at a crazy angle. A closer look revealed that it was the same problem as before – crumbling plaster. As they had pulled the wallpaper from around it, the fireplace itself had fallen out. So now we were without any heat in the living room.

Surveying the chaotic mess I wondered if we would ever be straight.

* * * *

Christmas week passed in a frantic whirl. Housework, cooking, washing, all were neglected to the constant traffic of the shop. We had enquired of all local builders, but no plasterer was available until after the New Year. Our only sources of heat now were the radiator in the kitchen and the gas fire in the bedroom. We had finally ceased struggling with the boiler and existed as best we could in the kitchen. The children, with Janet now on holiday from school, played in front of the bedroom fire and in spite of all our explanations asked repeatedly,

"When can we put up the Christmas tree?"

Finally, in desperation, Geoff got out our old artificial tree, put it up on the landing, and left the children to decorate it.

They kept it a secret, so as I wearily climbed the stairs to bed, it suddenly came into view in all its glory, beautifully decorated. I felt so thankful that even out of all this chaos, they had managed to create a bit of home and the magic of Christmas.

Chapter Five

Renovations and Renewals

Christmas coincided with a weekend that year, and I had eagerly looked forward to it as a well-earned rest. I would have time to get my bearings and perhaps unpack some of the suitcases and packing cases that still littered every room in the house.

Geoff, however, had other ideas. He was eager to do something about the dark, dismal appearance of the shop.

No sooner had I locked the door after a Christmas Eve during which I hadn't once sat down, than he began to clear the shelves.

"What are you going to do?" I asked.

"Paint, of course," he replied, and handed me a brush. "We can put one undercoat on tonight, another tomorrow, and the top coat on Boxing Day."

I set to work reluctantly, tired out, but as I saw the transformation wrought, even by undercoat, my spirits rose.

On Christmas morning, true to his word, while the children and I were exclaiming over our presents, Geoff painted away doggedly. It was not until the section of shelves he specified had received its second coat of paint that he agreed to get into the car and drive us back to Sheffield. There we were greeted warmly by parents and relatives. It was the first time we had seen them since moving in and they were naturally interested in how we were faring. We answered their many questions evasively and skilfully avoided asking them to visit us. We daren't let them see the lounge in its present state! An anxious moment came when Peter told his granny,

"We had to put the Christmas tree on the landing because the wall fell down."

"Oh, don't worry," I hastened to interrupt. "We didn't like the old fireplace so we've taken it out. We're having a new one put in." I hope sins of omission don't count too heavily against me in the next world.

On Boxing Day, after more painting, we allowed ourselves a very welcome rest. The following day we covered the shelves with blue Fablon. The finished result, with the white paint and blue shelves, was most impressive and brought much favourable comment from the customers when we re-opened after the holiday.

Unfortunately the sparkling new paint threw into horrid relief the rest of the shop, and fired Geoff with enthusiasm for more remodelling and redecorating.

After Christmas, trade in the shop became much quieter. We settled down to assess our position and decide what to do next. Our house in Sheffield was still not sold, so we were paying two mortgages and interest on a bridging loan from the bank. The stock in the shop was very low. Takings were pretty good, but we had only been there a month and had had no time to amass any capital.

We put this position to our chief grocery wholesaler, who very generously allowed us sufficient credit to restock properly. We were able to repay the loan a few weeks later when our house was finally sold, though at a lower figure than we had hoped. Lack of capital was a major drawback from the beginning, but it had its good points as it spurred us on to greater efforts of do-it-yourself.

Now life settled down to a routine of shop-keeping and painting. I seldom had a brush out of my hand. Gradually, the shop took on a lighter, brighter appearance.

Geoff became bosom friends with the woman who kept the paint and hardware shop higher up the village. I'm sure her takings must have soared by twenty per cent with all the paint that we bought. However, the shop was still rather dark, thanks to the large high backs to the windows which were built on and around the central heating radiators. We puzzled over the problem for some time. Finally one day Geoff came home:-

"I've found a handyman," he said, "He will take out the boiler and radiators for us, and offset their scrap value against the cost of replastering the lounge wall."

So we made the acquaintance of John Hudson. He arrived one morning a few days later, a young man, very well spoken. He was just starting up in business for himself. He was an excellent workman, quiet, efficient and considerate. We became firm friends, and a few days later, amid much banging, thumping and dust, we said a joyful farewell to the boiler.

Each night, after the children were in bed, we pulled down the blinds in the shop and set to work. The whole village was interested in our progress and people would stand outside, trying to see through the cracks in the venetian blinds. Little did they know that we could hear much of what they said through the partly open fanlight over the door. We often wondered why they didn't wait until morning, when they would be free to come inside and look around to their heart's content.

Now that the boiler and the radiators in the shop had gone, we were able to pull down the high backs of the windows. What a difference that made! At the grocery side we were able to push the frozen food counter into the space left by the radiators. Its shiny white back made a beautiful background for the goods we displayed in the small window area remaining. We applied a few more coats of white paint and re-arranged the counters and fridges. An obliging electrician installed an infra-red heater over the doorway, which kept the shop beautifully warm at the flick of a switch. He also installed an immersion heater which gave us constant hot water and we were finished. Late one night we dressed the grocery window with our latest and most tempting 'special offers'. In the drapery department we arranged a delectable display of knitting wool and patterns, all in the most delightful colours.

Then we pulled up the blinds, put on all the lights and went upstairs to our bedroom. There we hung the microphone of the tape recorder out of the bedroom window and sat down to await reactions. As the

37

nightly parade from the fish and chip shop passed below, we felt that all our efforts had been worthwhile. All the comments we overheard were favourable and we spent a hilarious evening trying to guess the identity of the unseen speakers below.

* * * *

Now that the shop was reasonably straight, Geoff turned his attention to the cellars. We desperately needed storage space for stock and since the cellars were beautifully dry, it was obviously sensible to use them.

The first one to be tackled was the 'boiler cellar'. This was comparatively easy. Geoff had one twin working with him to sweep up the enormous pile of dust and ashes. Together they would fill a bucket, which Geoff would then pass up through the cellar grate to the other twin waiting above. He would then empty this into the wheelbarrow and when this was full Geoff would climb up and push the barrow down to the bottom of the garden. As the twins' aim wasn't very good more of the ash went on the path than in the barrow. Then the return journey up the garden was enlivened by rides in the empty barrow, so progress was slow, but eventually the job was done. This cellar proved, when clean, to be light and airy, and we found it possible to get the children's bicycles and scooters down through the grating. We stored them there for the winter and the boys would play down there, having races over the smooth stone flags. Geoff also set up a tool bench here as there wasn't enough room in the garage and I was tired of having the kitchen used for such a purpose!

Now that the boiler was gone and the cellar clean,

it seemed possible to tackle the stock room from which it opened. This was very dark because the whole of the window had been boxed in to give a display area on to the street for the shop.

"Let's pull it down," I said, "surely we can put up some open shelves."

So once more, out came the saw and screwdriver and the high structure was pulled down. The result was amazing. The stockroom seemed twice as big. We painted it in a tasteful pink and managed to find room in it for the ice-cream fridge, which was still adorning the living room. The stairs which had previously seemed so dangerous were now quite simple to negotiate in the good light and became a useful short-cut to upstairs.

The other cellar was a very different proposition. For two solid weekends Geoff spent every hour down there. I heard bangs, thumps and thuds. Periodically he would appear with boxes and buckets of rubbish which he burnt down the garden. When he finally said, "Come and look", I could hardly believe my eyes. All the rubbish had disappeared, the long stone benches around the cellar had been whitewashed, the firewood and birdseed were neatly arranged each in its proper place and the whole room shone with cleanliness. We were able to bring down all the pet food and other canned goods that had overcrowded the stockroom and at times encroached on the living quarters.

"We're really getting somewhere at last."

A few days later the shop bell rang. It was John Hudson. "Right, Mrs. W. I've come to start on that wall," he said.

"Thank goodness." I led the way into the lounge. "If you need anything, just call."

"Mummy, can we help?" asked the twins.

"Yes, if you keep out of mischief," I replied.

The shop was busy and I had forgotten to order a small cob for the oldest inhabitant, a mistake that took a great deal of explaining, as she was extremely deaf. A distant sound of hammering came from the lounge, and dust began to thicken the air. I hastily shut all doors and carried on. Finally the boys came into the shop, covered from head to foot in a thick layer of dust.

"We're just chipping off the rest of the plaster, Mummy," they said.

Try as I would, I could not keep the dust out of the rest of the house. I consoled myself with the thought that the worst was nearly over and watched the boys loading plaster into their little barrow to cart outside with a light heart. Little did I know the worst was yet to come.

It was now the end of January and one morning John came to me and said,

"I'm starting the plastering today. Have you got a hose-pipe?"

"In the cellar", I replied. Imagine my horror when he fixed this to the tap in the kitchen, led it across the kitchen floor, through the hall, across the lounge, flung wide the front door and proceeded to soak the whole wall with jets of icy water.

Carefully keeping my voice neutral, I enquired what he was doing.

"Just wetting it down," he replied, "it makes a good key for the plaster."

The floor was a sea of mud, for the plaster dust still clung to it in spite of all my efforts at sweeping up.

For a whole week we lived with the front door open and all inside doors open to allow the passage of the hosepipe, while John alternately plastered and 'wetted down'. During this time the temperature outside never rose much above freezing and we had several light falls of snow.

At last the great day came. It was finished. The wall looked lovely, with beautiful pink plaster. John had also installed a gas fire to replace the old fire place.

The children worked hard all day sweeping and shovelling dust from the floor and after the shop closed Geoff and I donned our oldest clothes and started operation 'cleanup'. I scrubbed every inch of that floor three times over and still the plaster dust clung.

"Don't give up," Geoff kept saying as I clutched the table for support, swaying with weariness. "We've nearly finished."

At last it was clean. We would have to wait several weeks before decorating, to let the plaster dry out thoroughly, so we decided to use the room in the meantime. Joyfully we laid the carpet and phoned the gas company to come and connect up the fire.

"We'll come in a fortnight." we were told.

"We can't wait that long," said Geoff, "I'll fix it."

Once more the hosepipe was called into service. With the help of a tin of impact adhesive, Geoff connected it to the gas tap in the kitchen and the back of the radiator. Oh, the bliss of sitting in an easy chair in front of a warm fire!

The gas man's face, when he arrived two weeks later and saw the hosepipe snaking over the floor was quite a picture.

"Can't do that, love, it's against the law."

Chapter Six

Customers

By now we were beginning to know all our regular customers and, like all village shops, we had some strange characters.

One of the first to arrive in the morning, using the arrival of Jess and the bread van as a sort of unofficial clock, was Mr. Harris. His daily purchase was only one small milk cob, price sixpence, for he lived solely on his old-age pension. However, such is the force of a cheery smile and a regular order, that we valued his custom more than that of others who spent far more. Like many pensioners, his garden was his great love. During the summer months I was hard put to it to use all the lettuces and greenstuff which he lavished on me.

Later in the morning I would see a tall figure in a dark coat and shapeless green hat making her way up the street. Her progress was slow as she stopped for a word with everyone she met.

"It's Mrs. Wallace," I would call. "Rescue me in ten minutes." Another warm-hearted, cheery personality, Mrs. Wallace's opening words were invariably, "What's on offer this week, love?" Together we would consult the poster listing the reductions made by the wholesaler for that particular week. "I'll just take these love, and a tin of pilchards for the cat." She had endless difficulties with my surname, running the gamut of Wolstenholme, Woffindin, Wolfsterfield and many others, till I solved her difficulty by asking her to use my first name. After the manner of older people, she considered this a great privilege and we became good friends. Once she had done her shopping she would settle down to a long and heart-searching discussion of all her acquaintances. She knew the family history of everyone in the village and recited the long and complicated relationships of people who were complete strangers to me. She was a most useful mine of information and put me right many times when I was on the brink of making some dreadful gaffe like thinking two sisters were mother and daughter. She would stay and chat for hours if not interrupted, for she was a widow and rather lonely, so after about ten minutes Geoff would contrive to rush in with some emergency requiring my personal attention. I hope she never tumbled to our little dodge. She was one of our nicest customers.

Early in our occupation we got to know the local veterinary surgeon, a power to be reckoned with in the village. We were fortunate enough to have her custom and wished to keep it, for she ran a boarding kennel and bought a great deal of pet food, which carried a high profit margin. I had spoken with her on the telephone (she had a most cultured voice) and was amazed when I finally met her face to face. A large woman, sensibly dressed for her job, she wore a man's overcoat, trousers, and Wellington boots, the whole topped by a dilapidated red beret. She made a strange contrast to the city vets I was used to, in their white coats with collars and ties. I was at first shocked by the contrast between voice and appearance, for she smoked very heavily and seemed to have a cigarette permanently in her mouth. She insisted on punctilious service, but she bore all our many mistakes and omissions with great patience, only protesting violently if I forgot to include the inevitable packet of cigarettes in her order. A daily delivery was necessary for the kennels as pets were continually coming and going. Each evening about six-thirty we would hear an approaching rumble. "It's Keith", John and Peter would shout, racing for the door. Keith had a home-made barrow and was very popular with the twins, as he would give them rides in it whilst I assembled the order. Then the boys would stack the tins in the barrow, afterwards accompanying Keith part of the way back to Miss Weston's cottage and enjoying a ride in the barrow on the way.

Miss Weston's home-cum-surgery was a delightful cottage set in a lovely valley which we could see from the windows of the shop. Inside was a confusion of cages containing canaries, mice and budgies. Baskets containing convalescent dogs and cats stood in every corner and outside were goats, ponies and the kennels for the boarders. At surgery hours there was invariably a long queue stretching right up the garden path. Miss Weston had a heart of gold and made me a friend for life with her devoted care of our cat, when it swallowed poison twice in a week and nearly died.

Perhaps the oddest of our assortment of characters was Annie. A social misfit, the snippets we heard of her early life would have been sufficient to render her even odder than she was. She knew all the village gossip and as there was no love lost between her and

Mrs. Wallace we had to be very careful not to fan the flames of rivalry between them. We were told that they were distantly related, but they were not proud of the connection and neither would admit it. Annie had an unerring judgement as to the time we sat down to tea; no matter whether we ate early or late, as soon as we took our seats at the table, the shop bell would ring.

"Annie", we would groan in unison.

"Your turn."

"Oh, no, it's your shop!"

Finally one of us would stroll into the shop.

"I've brought this back," Annie would say, handing over an empty lemonade bottle.

"Thank you, do you want another bottle?"

"No. Just give me the threepence." (At this time it was still the custom to charge a deposit on drinks bottles, which could be reclaimed when the bottle was returned to the shop.)

Slowly scrutinising everything she passed, she would make her way to the door. Wearily we returned to our rapidly cooling tea.

"Ding". The bell again.

"Annie's back."

"Your turn this time."

Back into the shop again.

"I don't really know what I want," she would say gloomily surveying the cake counter. (We did, but it would not improve customer relations to tell her.)

"How much are the jam tarts?"

"Threepence ha'penny" (She knew as well as we did. This conversation was repeated every evening.)

"Got any of yesterday's?"

"One or two."

"How much?"

I'll let you have them for two-pence ha'penny. How many do you want?"

"Just one."

And she would produce the identical threepenny piece which I had given her half an hour earlier.

"It doesn't matter about the ha'penny. I'll take a Bell Boy (a cheap sweet) instead."

Once more she made her way slowly to the door. I followed as rapidly as was reasonably polite, anxious to lock up and return to my now stone-cold tea. As I dropped the latch, she would tap on the door.

"Just give me another bottle of pop, dear."

* * * *

Customers who bought knitting wool rapidly became friends. In common with most small shops at that time, we had a system of 'laying away' wool, the customer collecting one or two ounces per week as the work progressed. In the early days, when we did not know people's names, we identified them by their wool. 'That's the lady with the royal blue double-knitting', or 'the man with the brown double-double' (he collected for his wife on his way home from work).

This system of laying away wool caused us endless trouble and confusion. When a customer had chosen her wool it was placed in a large paper bag bearing her name and stacked on a shelf in the stockroom. Every time she called for more wool, it was necessary to sort through thirty or forty identical bags for the correct one. (Nowadays we would use colour-coded stickers to help identify things, but Sellotape was in its infancy and coloured stickers did not exist.) When the shop was busy, this sorting was no joke. It was reasonably simple with the good customers who called regularly for wool and collected it all within two or three weeks. However, we met the 'other sort' of customer. Typical is a lady who arrived shortly after we took over. After enthusing over the improvements we had made in the shop, and exclaiming at the delightful colours of our new stock, she finally picked a delicate pale green three ply.

"How much do you need?" I asked.

"Three ounces," she replied.

"Then that will be just six shillings please."

"Oh, no, I'll just take one ounce now and lay the rest away."

Four months later I was tidying the stockroom when I found the green wool at the bottom of the pile. With a sigh, I put it in the 'reduced' basket and it was quickly sold. The following week the lady reappeared asking for one more ounce of wool and was most annoyed to be told that it was no longer in stock.

"But you said you would save it!"

After this experience we put up a notice limiting the time we would save wool and were careful to draw customer's attention to it. However, we had become so used to this attitude that when someone asked for twenty ounces of wool and proposed to pay for it all there and then, I stared in amazement.

Nevertheless, the wool and drapery were my great delight. I never tired of rearranging the shelves to show the colours to best advantage and would stand for hours enthralled as customers leafed through the patterns and chose their wool. Many of them brought the finished garments in to show me and we would display them to any other customers who happened to be in the shop. Baby clothes were an especial joy as we happily planned the layette and when the new mother proudly wheeled the long-awaited baby up the village street, there was a double cause for admiration.

I was most touched also, to receive several offers to knit up the odd ounces of wool that I could not sell. Some of the women found time hung heavily on their hands and yet could not afford to buy wool to knit for themselves. They were only too glad to knit children's hats and mittens from the oddments of wool, without any charge, and I was able to sell these so cheaply that they found a ready market.

Two favourite customers were Mrs. Rodgers and her mother Mrs. Lawson. Joyce Rodger's daughter Susan was in the same class at school as Janet and they quickly became friends. Both Joyce and her mother made small purchases from us, but as they explained:-

"We both work for the shop next door, so we must buy our things from them."

In the past there had been great rivalry between the two shops, which more or less sold the same produce. These two ladies were very relieved that we felt no enmity towards our neighbours. It was some time before I actually met my counterpart next door, but relations were cordial and we were occasionally able to oblige each other with the loan of a few tins while waiting for the weekly delivery.

In all there were seven grocery shops in the village and the trade was shared fairly well between them. The co-operative stores, recently modernised, appealed most to the wives of miners and industrial workers and took the lion's share of the business. We other shops were patronised more by the farming community, who appreciated the personal service we offered. Competition was keen, and most shops belonged to one of the large buying groups, such as 'Mace' or 'Vivo'. This helped them to stand some sort of chance in competition with bigger stores and enable them to provide 'Special Offers' to tempt the housewives. Our predecessors had also introduced 'Green Shield Stamps' as another bait for customers – these were in their infancy and we had not previously come across them in the city.

My first morning in the shop comes vividly back to me.

"Twenty cigarettes please," a customer says. She puts the correct money on the counter.

"Thank you." I turn round from putting the money in the till and find that she is still standing there.

"Anything else?" I enquire.

"Stamps, please." Thanking she meant postage stamps, I looked blank, but she pointed to a book beside the till.

"It's one for every sixpence you spend, so I need six please."

Puzzled, I hand them over and seek enlightenment.

Nowadays, many supermarkets and filling stations have customer loyalty cards aimed at preventing 'shopping around'. Green Shield Stamps were available in many outlets, so gave little advantage in terms of customer loyalty – they were just another form of discount. We found that they cost us a considerable sum to buy, but since other shops also supplied them, they gave us little advantage in terms of trade. In the end, we decided to dispense with them. We lost a few customers, but felt that on balance we had made the right decision.

A newly-dressed window in a village excites a lot of interest from passers-by and we attempted to change ours once a week. Customers would discuss the rival displays while waiting their turn to be served. I listened with interest, and after dark, when the shop was closed, would slip out of the back door and wander up the village street, comparing and criticising.

All the shops relied heavily on visiting reps for their stock, the nearest warehouses being several miles away in the towns. Few shopkeepers were able to get away to visit them. The reps would call with special offers, saying that we should have the monopoly for a time, but actually selling to all the shops. When we found out that we were all carrying the same merchandise there were hard words for the reps on their next visit, when they would have a lot of returns on their hands. It was a very short-sighted policy on their part.

Chapter Seven

Winter in the Country

Early one morning towards the end of January, the children burst into our room.

"Mummy, it's deep snow outside and it's still snowing."

We dressed quickly and hurried to look out. As we opened the shop door a large pile of snow fell inwards on to the lino. The snow was very deep. We equipped the children with Wellington boots and warm clothes, armed everyone with shovels and set to work, making paths to shop, front and back doors and garage. As the drive was about fifty yards long it took Geoff and the children most of the morning to free the car. Luckily it was Saturday.

In the meantime I worried about the bread. Crich is on top of a hill and both approach roads have sharp bends, which could be very difficult in bad weather. It was Saturday and many people were depending on us for their weekend bread. Would Jess be able to get through?

I need not have worried. In the country they are prepared for such weather. Soon I saw the blue tractor from the farm at the top end of the village battling its way through the drifts towards the shop. Not long afterwards the yellow tractor from the other end of the village passed the door, and driving comfortably in its wake, only an hour later than usual, came Jess's familiar van. We gave him a hero's welcome of course, and he deserved it, for he had been out and about since 5am in order not to disappoint his many customers. One or two of the shops in the village did not receive their supplies of bread. Without exception they sold nationally advertised bread from the big bakery combines, which was delivered by townspeople who were easily dismayed by the bad weather.

Next day, as was our custom, we went over to Sheffield to visit our parents. After tea, my father switched on the radio for the news.

"Several Derbyshire villages have been cut off by deep snowdrifts since Friday," reported the announcer, naming ours amongst them. As we sat in the comfortable living room twenty miles away we thought of our uneventful journey and laughed heartily. We travelled home later that evening easily and without incident. I was amused to discover that my mother, in the city, had had to collect her milk from the dairy as deliveries had broken down due to the bad weather. We, in the country had received our milk only a couple of hours later than usual.

The snow did bring its worries, however. It fell for two or three days continuously and eventually the inevitable happened. The single power cable which supplied the whole village with electricity snapped. We had been warned that this was likely to happen and had laid in a good stock of candles. We sold these so rapidly that we had to institute rationing and had grave doubts whether our own supply would last out.

The shop looked like Aladdin's cave, with candles stuck on saucers all round the shelves. The children were thrilled and ran from room to room carrying guttering candles in their hands until I got so concerned about the risk of fire that all candles were confiscated and they had to manage by the feeble light of our one electric torch – not nearly such fun. We tried to obtain a paraffin pressure lamp, without success, but Geoff finally located a small lantern which gave only a feeble light but made life much easier and safer.

About an hour after the lights went out and the first rush and excitement was over, I began to be conscious of an unnatural silence.

"It's very quiet," I said to Geoff, "I wonder why?"

"The fridges aren't working," I suddenly realised.

"Well, did you expect them to work without electricity?" he replied.

This was a complication which had not previously occurred to me – I had been so busy worrying about the lack of lights that the lack of power had so far passed unnoticed.

We telephoned our suppliers. So far the phone wires were intact. "How long will the food keep?"

"Keep it covered and you should be safe for twenty-four hours," they replied.

We phoned the Electricity Board. When would the cables be repaired? They hadn't the slightest idea and gave us the impression that they didn't really care! As about fifty pounds worth of stock was involved, we certainly did care and kept a most anxious watch on the time.

Next morning came, after a rather disturbed night. We had found that we couldn't sleep without the noises of the fridges. Still no electricity. Frantically we phoned our suppliers.

"It's sixteen hours now. Can you do anything to help?"

"Sorry, we can't do anything," they replied. "All our vans are out on journeys and we can't contact them."

Another hour dragged slowly by. By now the ice in the fridges had begun to melt and soon the packets would be wet. We tried to rearrange them so that as few as possible would spoil. The shop door opened. It was our good friend George, with the week's grocery delivery.

"What's going on?" he asked, surveying the candles and lamp standing in readiness on counters and shelves.

Sadly we explained. "Perhaps I could help," he said, How much time have you got left?"

"Only about three hours, to be really safe," we replied.

"Let me see if there are any insulated boxes in the van."

We held our breath.

"Yes, it's all right." Thank goodness!

Quickly we transferred the packets and cartons to the insulated boxes and our kind friend drove back to his depot where they were stored in their huge refrigerators until our power supply was restored to us the next day.

We were never able sufficiently to express our

thanks for this timely help, for without it, our whole stock of ice cream and frozen foods would have been ruined.

Chapter Eight

The Knights of the Road

Now we began to be overwhelmed by dozens of commercial travellers. During the period before Christmas we had seen no one at all and at times I had been desperate to find sources of supply. We had decided that perhaps they considered us too small to bother with. We soon discovered our mistake.

The Christmas rush of trade was now over and all over the country Sales Managers were urging their men to push for bigger and better sales in the New Year. Thanks to my husband's job, I knew something of this from the traveller's side. Now I was to experience the shop-keeper's angle.

Some of the first to arrive were the 'Disinfectant boys', as we nick-named them.

"Buy now" they would say, "We have special discounts and you will be ready for the spring cleaning rush."

I explained that we had far too large a stock of

disinfectant already. This was something that had puzzled us for some time. We had case upon case of one particular brand. When we bought the shop, we had assumed that this brand must be very popular, but had found that it sold no more than other varieties. Although at that time we did not see the connection, we also had enormous quantities of talcum powder and shampoo. Sales were quite slow and we had reduced the price to well under cost in order to get rid of them. Now we were to find out the reason.

One day a smartly dressed gentleman came into the shop. He was wearing a tweed suit of the most dashing cut, a bow tie and a hat of the 'Robin Hood' type, which he raised most politely on entering. In his hand he carried an umbrella, which rather surprised me, for it was a ladies' umbrella.

"May I?" he asked, indicating the umbrella, and without waiting for permission, proceeded to unfurl it and presented it for my inspection. It was in the latest 'pagoda' style and was beautifully covered in two-toned green silk.

"Lovely job," he remarked.

I agreed, and waited for his next move.

"Would you like one?"

"They're not very useful in a shop," I hedged. If he was selling these things, I must be cautious. Not many housewives would have money to spare for such a luxury.

"Look, all you need to order is four cases of this, one case of that and two boxes of the toilet soap." He set a catalogue before me. I found myself gazing at pictures of the disinfectants and talcum powders which had cluttered my shelves for too long.

"No, thank you," I replied opening the shop door, "Good afternoon."

"But why?" he queried. "You can't go wrong with these, they're all excellent products."

I indicated the shelves behind him. "I don't dispute that, but we are already badly overstocked."

"Perhaps you would prefer a pair of sheets to the umbrella," he hazarded, but on seeing my face as I struggled to control my temper, he decided to give up and left hurriedly.

When he had gone, I put two and two together and remembering the smart umbrella which the daughter of the house had sported when we viewed the shop, I realised what had happened.

Later I was to find that this firm was not well thought of among the travellers. It's products were no more than average, but it managed to keep a high proportion of the market by dazzling gullible shopkeepers with 'free gifts'.

Most of the travellers we met were charming and helpful. The 'regulars' who supplied such staples as tea, cigarettes, eggs and of course, the 'potted meat man' all became firm friends. The 'pop' man again from a local firm, won the hearts of our boys when he allowed them to climb on his lorry and help to lift down the cases of lemonade and cider. Often, too, a 'free sample' found its way down their throats, and if they were at school when he called, an extra bottle would be left on the counter for them to 'try something new'.

Drapery travellers, although time-consuming, were a great delight to me. They would come through into the kitchen bringing perhaps five or six suitcases. Together we would unpack, admire and repack the goods.

I suffered agonies of indecision over the tempting goods spread before me, wondering what would appeal to the ladies of the village. I soon found that anything I liked myself was pretty sure to sell well. As far as children's clothing was concerned, I was fortunate, for I could order things which my own children were needing, in their own sizes and use these as samples from which to order others. I had to keep my purchases of drapery very low, for both cash and display space were severely limited, but the travellers were as polite and patient as if I were ordering in dozens rather than singles.

At first I was very nervous of the travellers representing big national concerns, such as biscuits, coffee etc. All had been trained in the 'high pressure' approach and had little appreciation of the problems of a shop-keeper who wanted a small quantity of several brands, rather than a lot of one brand. I found that firmness paid off and soon we were all on excellent terms.

One representative with whom I never really made friends worked for a nationally known firm of pet food manufacturers. He had so many 'special reductions', 'bonus offers', and new lines, none of which sold in our rather conservative community that I finally refused to buy at all. I found that I could get the few tins of his product that I really needed in half dozens from our local wholesaler.

In those days there was a great deal of duplication of effort in the grocery trade. Most wholesalers carried a very wide range of goods and were prepared to deliver in small quantities of half or one dozen. Very many manufacturers also had their own representatives. They offered better discounts than the wholesalers but would only deliver upwards of three cases at a time. So it often paid the retailer better to buy from his wholesaler rather than having capital tied up for a long time in relatively slow-moving stock.

The traveller for our toy wholesaler was another whom I welcomed with mixed feelings – not because of his manner, which was charming, or his wares, which were first-class – but because he always seemed to call outside school hours and the children would go mad with delight at the sight of his car.

Three eager faces would peer over the counter as he opened the first suitcase and there would be a rush to fetch tins and boxes to stand on, so as to get a better view.

"Oh, Mummy, this tractor is marvellous."

"What a pretty doll. Does it go to sleep?"

"That's only plastic. It won't last long."

"Please, Mummy, buy some of these guns. I want one."

"Don't forget a box of caps."

"Who is doing the buying around here?" I would ask, vainly struggling to get near the counter.

It was very difficult to turn something down, when three eager voices were clamouring 'I want one of those' just at my elbow. However, the children's tastes were a good guide to what would appeal to their age group.

All the children had pocket money with which they were able to buy a toy at cost price. Sometimes I would find myself saying, "Let me put the new stock in the window before you buy up the best things." We found however, that small boys would come into the shop asking for 'a spud gun like your Peter has', so on the whole the children did a wonderful job of free advertising for us.

Sweet travellers, also, were very popular with the

children. Many of them had sample cases of miniature bottles showing the full range of their wares and these certainly looked delectable spread out on the counter. As we only had space to display about a dozen jars of sweets at once, the choice was very difficult. We had to keep old favourites in stock, but longed to try something new. I'm afraid that just at first we sadly misled some of the sweet travellers. We gave them a large order and then spoiled it all by producing some of the dozens of empty jars which we had inherited and saying, "These will pay for the order."

Another regular was Bill, the egg man. Once a week, he delivered a case of eggs and also brought a bulk order from the girls at the egg packing station. Unfortunately they only bought the 'Special offers', and we found it very difficult to judge their requirements in advance. Sometimes we didn't have enough and sometimes we were left with stock on our hands, but we always looked forward to Thursdays as a sort of 'lucky dip day'. Would Bill bring us a good order or not? We never knew.

When we first decided to take the shop, dealing with travellers had been one of my great fears. By the time we left they had become old and trusted friends and I had certainly gained in poise and assurance.

Chapter Nine

The Joys of Spring

As spring approached and the weather grew milder, the children began to explore outdoors. Bicycles and scooters were hauled up from the cellar and off they went with their new friends. The garden soon proved a source of delight as it contained a small pond, little bigger than a puddle, which was full of frog spawn. The boys would spend hours gazing at this, hoping to see the tadpoles start to move. When, eventually the tadpoles developed into small green frogs they were highly delighted and would happily pass on a whole morning trying to catch the agile creatures. For the time being, however, we had a constant procession of small boys armed with jam jars, collecting a share of the tadpoles.

The garden outside the front door was soon a mass of green spikes as bulbs pushed their way through the earth, giving way to a delightful display of bluebells, hyacinths and daffodils under our windows. Whenever we could find a few moments we would be out in the garden, hoeing and weeding and exclaiming with delight as we identified new plants putting forth their leaves. I took advantage of the slack periods in the shop to sit in the garden in the sun. By leaving all doors open and sprinting at top speed as soon as I heard the bell, I could be behind the counter, only slightly out of breath, without causing the customer to wait more than a few seconds.

We discovered an old well by the garden gate, safely covered by a large millstone. The twins happily spent much time dropping stones through the hole in the middle of the millstone and listening to the splash far below. We were told that this well originally served the whole row of cottages and felt thankful that we had piped water.

There were many delightful walks within easy reach of the shop. One in particular took us along the top of a high escarpment from which magnificent views of the surrounding countryside were obtained. From the shop it was a steep climb up to the top of the ridge, but, once there, there were lovely level fields in which the children could run and play, while we sat and looked down on the village spread out like a model at our feet.

Nineteen sixty-two was the year when severe gales swept the whole of the country. With our usual luck, we were right in the path of one.

All day I had been running into the shop at the sound of the bell, only to find it empty, the door having been blown open by the strong wind. I was thankful when closing time came and I was able to lock up, but as the wind rose more and more, we became worried in case the hundred-year-old chimneys should come crashing through the roof. All night we lay and listened to the creaks, groans, bumps and thuds. Some of the noises were old familiar friends, but every few minutes a new squeak, whistle or bang would start and we would try to guess its cause.

Next morning we were all up early. From the living room window we could see a trail of broken telephone wire and shattered chicken coops all down the village street.

From somewhere over our heads, slates were sliding down into the garden with monotonous regularity.

"I'll go and see how bad the damage is," said Geoff. Choosing a moment between the falling slates he ran down the garden path.

"We've lost half the roof," he called.

I joined him at the gate. There was a huge gaping hole about ten feet square. We turned to look at the garage, a rickety wooden structure at the best of times. The whole of the back and one side was missing. The roof and the other side were resting precariously on the top of the car.

Just then the milkman came round the corner.

"I'll give you a hand with that," he called.

Gingerly Geoff crawled under the garage door and eased himself into the car. The milkman lifted the roof, Geoff drove the car rapidly out, and the whole structure collapsed with a tremendous crash.

We never managed to rebuild the garage. It had only been a wooden one, and the amount allowed by the insurance company just about covered the cost of carting away the rubbish.

The roof also caused us great anxiety as the type of tile required was no longer made. Our good friend, John Hunter, turned up trumps however, and after much searching located some on an old farmhouse that was being demolished.

After hearing some of the stories of gale damage

with which our customers regaled us for weeks afterwards, we congratulated ourselves on having escaped so lightly.

* * * *

One day an old lady came into the shop.

"I remember this shop when I was a girl," she said. "It was a hardware shop then and right in the middle of the floor stood a huge tank of paraffin. I still have a pair of vases bought from here as a present for my twenty-first birthday. Next month I shall be ninety."

She had been apprenticed to a dressmaker who had worked in what was now our bedroom. Later, when decorating the big walk-in cupboard in our room, we were thrilled to find a small metal case containing a set of three very fine crochet hooks. Did the dressmaker's apprentice drop them down a crack in the floorboards? We should never know. It would need a long apprenticeship to learn to crochet with such fine tools as these; I could just manage to work with the coarsest of the three, the others were far too fine for me to handle.

Our conversation with the old lady awakened our interest in the history of the property and we began to question our customers about it.

The building was originally three cottages, built in about 1820, of local stone. The outside walls were two feet thick. The cottages would have had one large living room downstairs, with a tiny kitchen behind. They were built back-to-back, so the kitchen would have had no window, and no running water. The kitchen did actually have a window (it still survived as a decorative feature of our house), but it gave only on to the living-room and very little daylight can have filtered through. There was a well by the gate, and an old brownstone sink (now full of rainwater at the bottom of the garden) had originally stood in the kitchen. The waste water had to be carried out to a drain in the garden.

The shop originally had only a small kitchen behind and a bedroom above.

About the 1920's however, the whole block of property came up for sale. The other cottages in the terrace were knocked two-into-one and bought by their tenants. The two end cottages were converted into one large house and connecting doors made into the shop. From this time, each succeeding owner had done a little more modernisation, but the original character of the building had fortunately been maintained. The change-over from hardware to grocery was fairly recent. In our opinion it had been a false move, for there were several other grocers in the village, but no hardware shop. During our tenure we tried, successfully I think, to build up the drapery and wool side of the business rather than the grocery.

In his spare time, Geoff had finally managed to wallpaper the lounge, and it now looked sparkling clean and fresh. Inspired by his success and spurred on by my constant grumbles, he now turned his attention to the kitchen. Although this had a large window, it was unfortunately overshadowed by a high stone wall. The gloomy effect was not improved by the decoration which consisted of beige tiles below and a mosaic wallpaper above in a tasteful scheme of black, red and yellow! The ceiling was deep yellow and the floor dark red. We had to keep the electric light burning all day.

Full of enthusiasm, Geoff started to peel off the wallpaper. In all he removed over thirty layers! About half way down was a layer of newspaper. We found a piece with the date – 1929! When we finally had it stripped I was sure the kitchen was an inch bigger all round. We didn't dare try to remove the tiles after our experiences with the plaster in the lounge and contented ourselves with painting them a cool, pale blue. Once more we used gallons of white paint for ceiling, woodwork and upper walls. The chimney breast of the kitchen was covered with the usual hardboard panel, concealing the usual monstrosity of a fireplace. This time, however, some use could be made of it, for in the shop we had unearthed an ancient gas fire, which Geoff installed in the fireplace, fitting a new hardboard panel round it. With new radiants this proved most effective and made the kitchen beautifully warm. When the decoration was finally finished the effect was so light and airy that we only needed to switch on the light on the very dullest days.

As the weather improved we became a favourite port of call for our friends and relatives from the city. We were delighted to see them, now that we had tackled some of the worst features of the shop, and proudly showed them round our new home. Luckily we never needed to worry about feeding them, for the shop provided everything and sometimes we joked that Sunday had the best takings of the week for my girl friends all fell for our displays of wool and insisted on buying enough to last until their next visit.

Spring in the country was delightful. We settled down to a peaceful pleasant routine and I felt as if I had been a shop-keeper all my life.

But as always, there was another bomb-shell just around the corner.

Chapter Ten

So Many Children!

John and Peter had been eagerly looking forward to Easter when they could start school. I too had looked forward to it, for they were always into mischief and I had continually to drop whatever I was doing to sort out quarrels and suggest new games. They both had a very strong sense of independence and there was not enough to occupy their interest at home. They needed the new challenge of school. At last Easter came and the boys settled down happily in school. However, instead of feeling a sense of freedom, I was terribly depressed. Continually feeling dizzy and ill, I dragged around the house and shop. Finally Geoff could stand my moping no longer and packed me off to the doctor.

"You're going to have a baby," she said.

As a mother of three, I should have realised, but I had been so busy I had never thought to look at a calendar!

This was a terrible blow and I became more depressed than ever. Running a shop with three children at school was one thing. Running a shop with a baby to feed every four hours, or a toddler with little fingers poking and prying was quite another. How would I be able to carry on? Would we have to sell the shop? Could we afford four children?

Geoff was a brick. "Don't worry. We'll cross one bridge at a time and manage somehow. I'll get you some help in the house and everything will be all right, you'll see."

And soon, everything was. Now I knew why I felt sick, it didn't seem too bad. From previous experience I knew it would soon pass. In the meantime, however, there were a lot of arrangements to be made. I telephoned the doctor.

"Can you help me, doctor? I know I have to have a monthly check-up, but if I come to your regular ante-natal clinic, everyone in the village will know I'm pregnant and this may be bad for business."

"That's all right, Mrs. W. I've met your problem before. I have a surgery in the next village. Come and see me there."

So for the next three months I travelled four miles each way in order to keep my secret.

Imagine my horror when I discovered that the doctor's very charming receptionist, who had been in on the secret from the start was the daughter-in-law of our 'rivals' next door!

No one in the village suspected, however, and I was very grateful to her for keeping the secret so well.

* * * *

Since just after Christmas, I had had the help of a 'daily' to do some of the cleaning for me. Mrs. Marvel certainly lived up to her name and manfully tackled the enormous piles of washing which we delivered to her house on Saturday afternoons and which she duly returned, all ready for ironing, on Monday afternoons. The problem of transporting so much washing was easily solved – she put it all in an old pram and cheerfully pushed it up the village street.

She also came two other mornings a week to do some of the heavier cleaning and relieve me of the almost impossible job of cleaning the bedrooms when the shop was open.

Mrs. Marvel had three children; a small daughter and two boys a little older than John and Peter. These four made each other's acquaintance at school and soon became firm friends. Unfortunately for my peace of mind, a 'gang' soon developed. My two were the youngest and they would go off for hours exploring the countryside for miles around. They would come home wet, dirty and tired, but grew strong and healthy so I tried not to worry too much.

A serious scrape soon occurred, however. Our stock of sweets and cigarettes was kept in a stockroom accessible from upstairs, the living room and the shop. Suddenly our sales of these commodities seemed to have risen and I found stocks were running short. This state of affairs continued for about two or three weeks.

Then one morning I heard a call from Mrs. Marvel who was cleaning the bedrooms.

"Mrs. W., come and look at this."

She had moved away the hardboard cover from the hideous old fireplace in the boys' bedroom, intending to clean behind it. But there, in neat stacks, were about two hundred cigarettes and a varied assortment of sweets. She had obviously found the boys' secret hoard.

When they came home from school, we tackled them. In order to keep in favour with the bigger boys in the gang, who didn't want 'tinies' tagging along, they had been making them presents of our sweets and cigarettes. They had even tried smoking the cigarettes, but luckily had coughed so much that they hadn't tried again.

A long lecture ensued, which must have done the trick, for we had no further trouble of this kind. For our part, we tried to make home more attractive and to spend more time with them so that they did not need to seek excitement with the older boys.

For a few weeks there was peace. Then the weather grew warmer and the days longer and the boys were tempted further afield once more. During the Whitsuntide holidays they were out every day.

"Where are you going?" I asked.

"Oh, we've got some new friends and we're playing at making a tent with them."

This seemed harmless enough and all seemed well.

They had been back at school two days when the phone rang. It was the school headmistress.

"I'm sorry to have to tell you that your boys have dirty heads."

"But I wash their hair regularly!" I replied, naively.

"No, you misunderstand me. They have lice in their hair."

I was utterly disgusted, for I had never experienced such a thing. Luckily the school authorities were extremely helpful (there proved to be an epidemic in school) and with the help of a most efficient shampoo, their heads were clear within a few days.

With help from the teachers I found out the cause of the infection. The boys' 'new friends' were the village 'down-and-outs', and the close, cramped quarters of the 'tent' had made the infection inevitable.

Once more we tried to keep the boys at home, but we began to worry. Were they suffering through lack of supervision?

At the end of the summer term all parents were invited to the 'Open Day' at school. Luckily this was on a Wednesday afternoon, our half day closing, so I was able to attend. Each class was to give a short concert. As I spoke to the headmistress beforehand she said,

"We've made it easy for you, Mrs. W. Janet will be reciting early in the programme. If you stay to hear her, you can move into John and Peter's classroom during the interval for they will not be performing until the second half.

I gave her full marks for consideration. Although it was only a small school, not many teachers would have gone to so much trouble to see that mothers of more than one child were able to see all their children's performances.

It was a most delightful afternoon and I came home comforted to see my children so happy with their teachers and classmates.

* * * *

Quite early on, Geoff, worried about my being left alone so much, had told Jess, the baker's roundsman, of my pregnancy.

"Don't you worry, Mr. W. I'll see she's all right," he had said. From then on, he never forgot to ask if I needed anything lifting.

"All right for sugar and firewood?" he would ask. Sugar came in parcels of 28lbs and had to be carried from the stockroom. Firewood was sold by the sack and came from the cellar.

Jess was a real tower of strength. He was not much given to conversation and I had to work hard to draw him out, but soon discovered that he was quite well travelled. As he was a native of Derbyshire with a strong local accent, I was amused and surprised to hear the occasional few words of French slip out. In our chats over the inevitable morning tea I discovered that during the war he had met a Belgian girl and had returned after the war to marry her. They now had three children, two boys in their teens and the 'Baby' as he called her, now three years old. Each year the whole family went over to Belgium to visit the wife's relatives. Consequently Jess spoke fluent French, though his local accent was so strong it must have puzzled the Belgians at times. He was very proud of his family and kept us amused and the twins enthralled, with the tales of his own two boys.

By the end of the summer my condition was becoming obvious and I decided the time had come to tell the children. They were delighted, especially Janet, who immediately put in a request for a little sister.

"Two boys are quite enough, Mummy."

They speedily told all their friends too, and soon the shop bell would ring and a smiling face would say:-

"Our Kevin says there's to be an addition to your family. Is it true? I'm so pleased."

For a while all was peaceful. I began to assemble a layette. Delighted to have a genuine excuse, I collected bundles of all the most daintily coloured baby wool, pored over patterns and finally started knitting. After five years, I had disposed of all previous baby equipment and now needed everything new. What an excuse for a spending spree! I delighted in ordering little dresses and rompers, ostensibly to sell in the shop, but having the thought at the back of my mind, "If it doesn't sell I can always use it myself." It was a great saving to be able to buy nappies (no disposables in those days!) and nighties at cost price and for the first time in any of my pregnancies I actually had a variety of maternity smocks.

We didn't believe in spending a lot on babies, however, so as always, I cut down old blankets and sheets to cot size and bought a second-hand cot from someone in the village.

One morning a customer parked a pram outside the shop window and came inside.

"Is this pram any use?" she said. "I've finished with it. You can have it for nothing."

The long summer days passed happily, the children were not at school and at every opportunity we would pack up sandwiches and take them out into the fields. Even a trip as far as the bottom of the garden was something of a treat for me after being tied to the shop all day.

One place in particular seemed like paradise to the children. Only a mile or two from our village, at Cromford, was a large open meadow. It was bounded on one side by a river and on the other by a busy railway line. We could picnic here and watch the trains pass. On the third side was the local cricket ground, where matches were often in progress. Geoff and the boys would watch them happily for hours. The great delight, however, was a very large, level stretch of tarmac, completely enclosed from the road, where as a very great treat we allowed them to steer the car, sitting on Geoff's knee and executing the most complicated turns as he drove slowly along in first gear.

With excursions like these, and visits to grandparents, the summer holidays seemed to fly past.

Chapter Eleven

Gathering Clouds

Small clouds were beginning to gather on the horizon. We had had to change our grocery wholesaler. The new delivery man was not so obliging as our old friend Graham had been and dumped everything in the middle of the shop floor. Geoff had never actually served in the shop, except occasionally on Saturday's, but he had been extremely helpful in lifting heavy packing cases and boxes behind the scenes. Now his work was taking him away from home more and more and I found that I was having to do much more heavy lifting myself, in spite of Jess's help. I daren't tell the doctor that I had been lifting 28lb parcels of sugar, but she knew something was wrong, all the same. In no uncertain terms I was told that I must rest more.

In an effort to help me take things more easily, Geoff engaged Glenda to come and serve in the shop for three mornings a week. She proved to be a real treasure, capable of turning her hand to anything and became yet another valued friend. She not only served and kept the shop clean, but would iron, sew, clean or cook as the need arose. She had one child, a little girl, the same age as the twins and all the children became good friends. But it still wasn't enough. I still became tired and yet the shop takings were not sufficient to warrant any more outside help.

Then came one night which really frightened me. Geoff was away as usual on business and I was, as usual, alone with the children. About four o'clock in the morning I awoke with a start. I lay, listening, wondering what had disturbed me. I heard nothing and was just dozing off again when I was jerked once more into consciousness. The back door handle was being rattled. Telling myself firmly, 'It's only the wind!' I tried to go back to sleep. But I knew very well there was no wind. At intervals the noise continued. Then I heard the sound of footsteps rounding the corner of the house. Quickly slipping out of bed and hurrying to the window, I was just in time to see the figure of a man walking off down the street. The light from the one street lamp was very feeble and it was not yet daylight, but I could see that he was wearing a cap and from his rather bent walk, seemed to be elderly rather than young. Perhaps he had been for cigarettes, though it seemed much too early for that. Also, if he had been a miner on his way to work, he would have been going in the opposite direction. I breathed a sigh of relief and climbed back into bed. Before I had time to get to sleep however, I heard the footsteps returning. Once more the door handle rattled. And again, and again. By this time I was thoroughly frightened. Most people knew that my husband was away, and a shop is always a tempting bait for a burglar, although we never kept much money in the house. I knew that both front and back doors were securely locked, but what about the cellar? Both cellars had outside gratings which could be easily lifted from outside. The doors leading from cellar to house each had strong bolts, but I couldn't remember if they had been fastened. One cellar grating was right beside the back door. I listened anxiously for the sound of the grating being pushed back, but this didn't come.

Once more I climbed out of bed and stood hesitating on the landing. Should I go down and see if the cellar doors were fastened? Unfortunately the stairs were right opposite the back door, which was glass and I could not go downstairs without running the risk of being seen. If I went down and the intruder realised I was alone, he might not hesitate to break down the door. Alone in the darkness, I began to imagine all kinds of terrible things. Finally I pulled myself together. It would be another hour at least until daylight and the man would not be content to fiddle with the lock on the door much longer.

Gathering all my courage, I decided to risk the other staircase, which was very steep and winding. I crept slowly down the narrow stairs in the inky blackness. I dare not put on a light, and groped my way to the telephone. Of course, the lady who ran our local exchange was in bed, and as I waited for her to answer, the noises from the back door seemed to get even louder. Finally she answered and connected me to the police station.

"I'll come up at once," said our kindly local bobby when he had finally wakened sufficiently to understand what I was trying to tell him, "but I'm afraid there's little chance of my catching him."

I think the next twenty minutes were some of the longest of my life. How relieved I was to see the dim glow of the approaching policeman's torch. As he drew closer and the sound of his feet became audible, the noises from the kitchen stopped and the intruder presumably made off down the garden, for he was gone by the time the policeman arrived. Although he made a thorough search, he could find nothing, but the country behind the shop was such that a man could easily have got away without being seen, particularly as it was a moonlit night. As for me, I turned on every light in the house, drew all the curtains tight and settled down to do the week's washing. The children were somewhat startled to come down at seven o'clock to find me taking the last load out of the washer, but the hard work had calmed my nerves wonderfully.

When Geoff came home at the week-end and heard my story, he was most concerned. "This won't do. What if you had fallen on those dark stairs and the baby had started early? No-one would have heard you call out. I must get you to 'civilisation' again.

The more we talked it over, the greater the difficulties facing us appeared. I was now rather nervy and depressed and from this time on, never slept straight through a night without waking. I should be out of action for at least a month at the time of the baby's birth, which, being Christmas, would also be our busiest time in the shop. For at least three months afterwards I would probably need full time help in the shop. The takings would not cover this extra expense and we had not had sufficient time since moving in to build up any savings.

Finally, and reluctantly, we decided. We would sell the shop.

Chapter Twelve

The Other Side of the Picture

It was hard to decide to sell the shop. It was even harder to actually do it.

All the reasons which had been given to us for buying it now became difficulties in selling:-

'Delightful country village' became 'Isolated country backwater.'

'Easy to run single-handed' became 'No scope for expansion.'

'Spacious living quarters' became 'Draughty barn.'

'Large garden' became 'Uncultivated wilderness.'

First of all we went to see the estate agent who had sold us the property twelve months previously.

"What are you asking for it?" he enquired.

We named the sum that we had originally paid.

"That's far too high. You'll have to knock five hundred off. (This was at a time when an average semi-detached house sold for about £2000.)

We pointed out that a year ago it had been 'dirt

cheap at the price' and that we had made tremendous improvements both in equipment, decoration and turnover.

"Well. I'll try," he finally said without enthusiasm.

We waited for five weeks during which he did not send a single person to view the property.

In desperation we decided to have a go at selling it alone. Thinking that there must be other city people like ourselves who wanted to live in the country, we advertised in the Sheffield papers. This produced a flood of phone calls, but most people thought we were too far out and didn't bother to pursue the matter further.

Time was beginning to run out. I was seven months pregnant and we had not progressed at all. We decided to try another estate agent. Certainly this one took his job more seriously and we began to get more enquiries. Each time someone asked to visit Glenda, Mrs. Marvel and I would fly around getting everywhere into apple pie order.

We had all sorts of enquiries. Old people wanting somewhere to which they could retire (far too big). Young couples without children wanting an extra income (too far from centres of entertainment). Couples with children wanting an extra income (too much hard work).

Time flew past and still we hadn't found the right people. I stopped frantically tidying up every time someone came to view. We started re-ordering stock, which we had allowed to run down in order to lower the price of the business. I became convinced that I should still be a shopkeeper when the baby was born and made arrangements with the local midwife.

One Monday morning I was frantically busy. Mrs.

Marvel had given in her notice the week before, quite unexpectedly. I think she had become fed up with the uncertainty of not knowing how much longer her job would last and had been offered a more permanent job elsewhere. She would not admit this, just stating flatly that her husband didn't want her to work any more. Glenda couldn't come on a Monday. I left all the housework, which was considerable as we had been out all the previous day. There was a great deal of clearing up to be done, but I decided to concentrate on the shop and the washing.

I had stripped the beds before the shop opened. I sorted the clothes into untidy piles of whites, coloureds, woollens etc. all over the kitchen floor and put the first load into the washer, a twin-tub, very efficient but prone to splashing if overloaded, which it often was.

The shop bell rang. It was a traveller. There were quite a few things that I needed and the shop was quite busy so that it was after 11.30 when he left. I raced back into the kitchen. The children would be home for lunch in less than half an hour, nothing was prepared and I hadn't even started the washing.

Hastily peeling some potatoes, I popped them on the gas as the bell rang once more. I hurried back into the shop. A couple stood there.

"May we see round the shop, please?"

I was in too much of a hurry to go through my usual 'selling' routine. Mumbling an apology for the mess in the kitchen and bedrooms, I left them to find their own way around the building.

"If you have any questions, could we talk in the kitchen please?" I asked.

So they perched uncomfortably on stools and shouted their questions over the noise of the spin dryer while I hastily prepared the lunch and rushed in and out of the shop serving the mothers on their way up to collect the children from school. Then our children came home for lunch and I thankfully bid my visitors goodbye.

When Geoff came home at the weekend there were so many other things to tell him that I quite forgot to mention this incident. Consequently when the phone rang, Geoff answered it and was told

"Mr. & Mrs. Morgan want to buy the shop."

"Whoever are they?" he asked.

Completely stunned, but very thankful, I explained. The estate agent later told me that they had thought it seemed a busy little shop (which it was) and that if I could cope with so much chaos when seven and a half months pregnant, it would be as easy as falling off a log for them.

Chapter Thirteen

On the Move Again

We may have sold the shop, but our troubles were not yet over. For several more days we lived on tenterhooks while the prospective buyers made up their minds whether they could afford our price. The country was still in the middle of a credit squeeze and we carried rather a lot of stock. Finally however, we persuaded our wool wholesaler to take back a great deal of the unopened stock of wool. We promised also to cut down other stock as much as possible and finally got the price down to a satisfactory level.

We had high hopes that Mr. & Mrs. Morgan would make a real success of the shop. They were a young couple with only one child – a little boy. Like Geoff, Mr. Morgan intended to carry on his job (he was a miner), but unlike me, Mrs. Morgan would have constant help in the shape of her parents, who lived with them. We became quite friendly and did all we could to make the transfer easy and pleasant.

Now the old familiar routine started again. Slowly, a little at a time, I started to empty drawers and cupboards and a pile of boxes and cartons grew steadily in the boxroom.

By this time it was the end of October and the shop was becoming very busy with the build-up towards Christmas. My husband was becoming more and more anxious about my health – the baby was due on 20th December. Geoff constantly harried the solicitors to speed matters up. Finally they listened to his pleas and moving day was fixed for November 12th.

One Sunday we had a field day. We collected all the cardboard boxes we could find and set to work.

"We've got to reduce the stock, so you may as well enjoy yourself," said Geoff.

We went round the shelves taking tins of this and that, buttons, needles, hairgrips, furniture polish, everything that we could conceivably need for months to come.

I laid in a supply of children's underwear and socks in gradually increasing sizes. I also packed what seemed like mountains of wool which later was used up with great rapidity.

When we had finished, every inch of the spare room floor was covered in boxes and cartons. The shelves in the shop looked very bare and empty, but we had just about reduced it to the required figure.

By now I was frantically busy once more. Glenda and I between us were running the shop, doing all the housework, preparing and cooking meals, sorting and packing. In addition I was making lists for Mrs. Morgan of customers, travellers and wholesalers and trying to prepare my Christmas presents well in advance. Mrs. Morgan had asked me to order Christmas stock on her behalf, to be delivered after we had gone. It was rather nerve-racking to have the responsibility of spending someone else's money, but it was lovely to have the fun of ordering all the delectable Christmas lines which I had had to refuse up to now.

With all these worries on my shoulders, I now added one more – the greatest of all. We had sold the shop, but where were we going to live?

Once more we had picked winter for our move. There were very few houses for sale in our price range and the credit squeeze was as bad as ever.

Geoff was spending every spare moment visiting estate agents in the city, looking for a four bedroomed house with all the bedrooms on the first floor. There were a few to be had, but all around the six thousand pound mark – way beyond our reach.

November came and I had visions of having the baby on the pavement. Our parents had offered us accommodation, but neither had sufficient room to take all of us and a new baby is not the ideal visitor for elderly people.

At last, two weeks before we were to move out, Geoff came home with some good news.

"I've found a house. The decorations are bad, but it has four bedrooms and it is reasonably modern. I'll take you to see it on Saturday."

We arranged for Glenda to look after the shop on Saturday afternoon and towards tea time we set off. It was dark before we reached Sheffield. Geoff drew to a halt in a pleasant looking street on the outskirts.

"This is it."

All I could see was a very high privet hedge.

He led the way to the front door. The house was unoccupied but still furnished. All the lights were very dim and the furniture big and old fashioned. The decorations were appalling, but we were used to that.

The rooms were a good size, however, and conveniently arranged. Above all there was a large, dry cellar, with several rooms, which would take all Geoff's tools and his beloved electric train.

We couldn't see the garden as it was dark, but there was a lovely view over the city with its myriad twinkling lights.

"Let's take it."

"Good."

I heaved a sigh of relieve. At least the baby would have a roof over its head. I leaned back in my seat and listened to the chatter behind me as the children discussed the house and its many wonders. Even in the dark they had managed to locate a swing and a sandpit. They argued over which bedrooms they would have.

Only another week to go.

The hectic round of shop, pack, house, food, bed, continued. I tried not to worry about the conditions at our new house – there wasn't a cooker, we had no doctor or home help lined up and the telephone had been disconnected. Once again, it was a race against time.

Finally the last weekend was upon us. Giving the children yet more cardboard boxes, we suggested they should pack their toys and the Morgans and I repaired to the shop to start stocktaking.

It all seemed so familiar. "Eleven pairs of seam-free nylons at 4/11. Five pairs fully fashioned at 7/11. Five dozen assorted reels of cotton. Nine dozen assorted embroidery silks. Three hundred and fifty knitting patterns at sixpence."

At least this time things were in order and the work went with a swing. Geoff and I had counted and priced many things beforehand so that in an amazingly short time we had everything listed.

The Morgans, however, were exhausted.

"We'll come back tomorrow to price it all out."

"Come early, it's a long job."

"We'll be there by ten o'clock."

Ten o'clock came and went, but there was no sign of the newcomers. Geoff and I settled down alone to the long and tiring job of pricing. By lunch time it was half done.

A knock came at the door. Mr. & Mrs. Morgan at last.

"This is what we've done so far. Perhaps you would like to check our figures."

"Oh, no, we'll take your word. It's sure to be all right."

By eleven o'clock that night it was all finished, a price agreed, and once more, we shook hands on the sale of a shop.

For us, it was a sad moment.

Chapter Fourteen

Exit

Moving day, and we were up bright and early. The removal men and the first customers arrived together.

"Just come to say goodbye, dear. I've brought you a little something to remember me by."

"Excuse me please, but could you come and show us which things you will be taking with you?"

Hastily I thanked my kind friend and hurried out of the shop to show the removal men around. All seemed straightforward downstairs.

"Everything from all these bedrooms must go," I said, opening each door in turn.

"Yes, that's all right," said the removal man, following on my heels.

Then I opened the door of the spare bedroom. The man stood transfixed as he gazed at the wide expanse of floor completely hidden by boxes and crates of every size and shape.

"And all this too," I said and rushed away quickly as the shop bell came to my rescue, leaving him staring sadly into the equally crowded boxroom.

All morning the shop echoed to the thumps and

bangs of the removal men as once more they struggled with our large furniture on the narrow stairs.

All morning the shop bell rang continually as people called in to wish us good luck and God speed.

"Don't forget to write and let us know whether it's a boy or a girl."

"Do come and see us and bring the new baby."

Lunch time came, and with it the sound of a horn outside. The Morgan's furniture van had arrived. Chaos reigned for a while, but soon a system was evolved and work proceeded apace, loading our van from the front door and unloading the Morgan's van at the back door.

I had intended to make some sort of picnic lunch in the kitchen, but with so much coming and going it was impossible. Geoff stepped into the breach.

"Get into the car," he said. "You're going out for lunch."

So we all piled into the car and were driven off to enjoy a delightful lunch in the peace and quiet of a restaurant in the nearby town. Much refreshed, we returned to the fray, to find our van packed and the removal men finishing their sandwiches.

"Come along, it's time to go."

I collected Tipsy the cat from the room in which we had shut him during the packing process, so that he would not run away, and wandered for the last time through the familiar rooms.

It didn't seem like home any more. Already the house was taking on a different aspect as the Morgan's furniture was moved in.

I wandered into the shop where I had spent so many happy hours. Already Mrs. Morgan was at home there, and was helping a customer choose some wool.

"Goodbye, dear, have a good rest. The best of luck when the baby come."

A horn blew warningly outside. Geoff was waiting in the car, with the children bobbing excitedly up and down in the back seat.

"Come on, Mummy, hurry up."

I got into the car. The removal van set off in front.

"Goodbye, goodbye."

One last look at our names above the door, and we were off on our way to a new adventure.

Chapter Fifteen

Post Script

It is Christmas day. The house glows with light and warmth. In the kitchen, ably assisted by mother and aunt, I cook the Christmas dinner. The baby is very much overdue, but I'm hoping it doesn't arrive today. Upstairs John lies in bed, suffering from measles and very upset because he feels too ill to eat roast turkey. In the sitting room a crowd of other relatives combine to entertain Peter, just recovering from measles, and Janet, just starting. A ring on the doorbell. It is the doctor to see the sick children.

He glances at my apron, the frantic activity in the kitchen, the crowds of people and the sick children. He opens his mouth to speak, sees my happy face, sighs and shakes his head.

"You really must try to rest more, Mrs. W." he says.

* * * *

New Year's Eve. Christmas merrymaking is over and I am wrapped in gloom. I have almost persuaded myself that I am not pregnant and that it was all some horrible dream. I am so depressed that we do not even stay up to see in the New Year, but go to bed early. I wake just before midnight and gloomily watch the hands creep past twelve. It's 1963, and still no baby. Then suddenly I catch my breath and start to watch the clock. This is it. I wake Geoff and call the midwife. We make all the preparations and at 1.30 the midwife arrives, panting. It is deep snow outside and her car repeatedly got stuck in drifts. By this time I was pretty uncomfortable. Immediately setting Geoff to work to make a cup of tea, she set about her own preparations. At 2am, "The baby's coming," I gasp.

"Don't be silly, dear, it can't be coming yet."

But it is. Ten minutes later she is born. Susan Mary, a beautiful little girl.

"What a wonderful way to see the New Year in," says Geoff coming in with the tea.

Printed in Great Britain
by Amazon